Kids Word Cookbook

Scott Ravede

Kids Word Cookbook by Scott Ravede

ISBN: 978-1-7348671-0-7 – Case Laminate
978-1-7348671-1-4 – Paperback
978-1-7348671-2-1 – Kindle
978-1-7348671-3-8 – eBook

Scott Ravede Books
Scott@ScottRavedeBooks.com
www.ScottRavedeBooks.com

Disclaimer: Eating your words is a figure of speech, and not meant to be taken literally, and following the recipes in the back of this book will not actually result in edible food.

Special note: Check out the "wordy" recipes in the back of this book, so you can see how these dishes were made. But kids, please don't touch the kitchen utensils without your parent's permission.

Illustration: Rivka Ravede / rivkaravede73@gmail.com

Design / Layout: Rik Feeney / www.RickFeeney.com

Get ready to eat your words.

Regular food is for the birds.

Don't be a dummy.

Forget about your tummy.

Pay attention to your vocal cords,

And get gorging on some lo-cal words.

By digging into these fine recipes,

You'll have more fun

than the flies and the fleas.

I have a fly.
My fly flies high.
How high does my fly fly?
My fly flies so high,
I call him my High Fly fly.

I have another fly.
All this fly does is lie.
He lies so much,
I call him the Lie Fly fly.

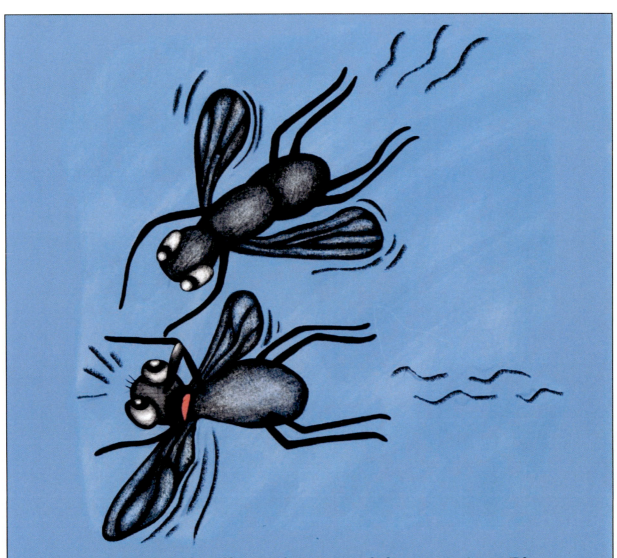

High Fly flies down and lies on Lie Fly.
Lie Fly spies High Fly on Lie Fly and flies high.

Lie Fly lies in lye pie with lye flies.

Lie Fly dies from lye in lye pie.

High Fly flies by Bea in the sky.
Bea is a bee that does not fly high.
High Fly wants Bea to be a fly,
and fly as high, as High Fly flies.

Bea does not want to be a fly,
or fly as high as High Fly flies.

Bea the bee wants
to be a bee,
and tells High Fly
to let her be.
So, when High Fly says,
"fly high, fly high,"
Bea the bee
just says, "Good Bye!"

I have a fly whose name is Flea.
I have a flea whose name is Fly.
Flea the fly flies to Fly the flea.
Fly the flea flees from Flea the fly.

Why?

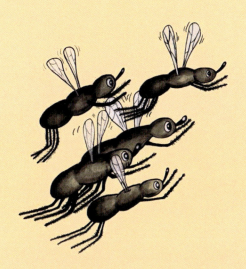

Flies fly to fleas.
Fleas flee from flies.
Is that wise?
Let's go ask the Y's.

Here are the Y's.
The Y's are wise.
Who knows why the Y's are wise?
The Y's know why the Y's are wise.
Why do the Y's know the Y's are wise?
Because the Y's are wise, that's why.

What about the fleas and the flies?
The wise Y's know why the flies fly.
The wise Y's know why the fleas flee.
But they are not telling you,
and they are not telling me.

Some holes have moles. Some holes do not.
The holes that have moles are holes that are wholesome.
The holes that do not are holes that are lonesome.

If some moles loan some moles to the holes
that are lonesome,will the holes
that are lonesome,then become wholesome?

A lone mole lives alone
in a lone hole.

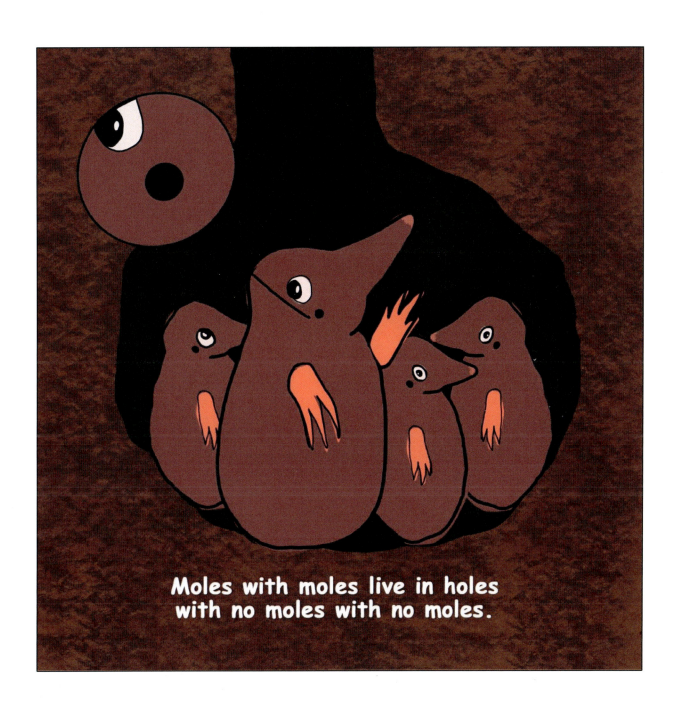

Moles with moles live in holes
with no moles with no moles.

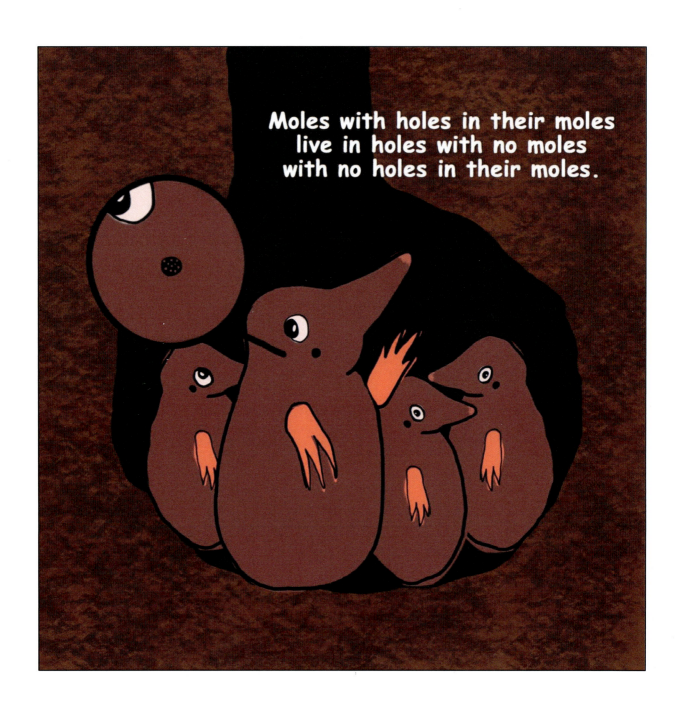

A sole mole meets a lone mole
in a troll hole.
Now no more sole mole nor lone mole
in the troll hole.

You have a gnu.
Once it was new.

Read a red book and make that red book read.
Read a blue book and make that blue book read.

One read red book and one read blue book
make two books that are read.
One blue and one red.

Questions for Kids Word Cookbook

1) If you could eat your words, what do you think they would taste like?

2) Do you think you would get full, or would you gag on the words instead?

3) Do you think anyone would really make a pie out of lye?

4) Would Lie Fly really be able to lie in the sky or on a cloud?

5) How high do you think flies can really fly?

6) Have you ever seen flies fly to fleas or fleas flee from flies?

7) Why do you think the Y's wouldn't tell what they knew about flies and fleas?

8) Do some moles really have moles on their faces?

9) Did you know that another word for gnu is wildebeest? Which name do you like better?

10) Where do you think gnomes come from?

11) Do you live closer to Nome or Rome? In which place would you feel more at home?

12) In Red Books and Blue Books was it hard to keep track of whether the word "blue" was a color or a feeling of sadness? Were you getting "red" mixed up with "read?"

13) Did you find yourself pronouncing "read" like "red" when it should have been pronounced like "reed?" And vice versa?

Glossary

Alliteration: repetition of usually the first consonant sound in 2 or more words close together

Assonance: repetition of the same vowel sound in 2 or more words close together

Circular Reasoning: occurs when the end of an argument comes back to the beginning without having proven itself

Consonance: repetition of the same consonant sound in 2 or more words close together

Heteronyms: words that are spelled the same but have different pronunciations and meanings

Homonyms: words that are pronounced and spelled the same but have different meanings

Homophones: words that are pronounced the same but have different spellings and meanings

Heterographs: words that are pronounced the same but have different spellings and meanings

Homographs: words that are spelled the same, may or may not be pronounced the same, but have different meanings

Mondegreen: a word or phrase resulting from a mishearing of another word or phrase

Oronyms: different words or phrases that sound the same

Reverse Oronyms: 2 sets of words or phrases in which each set is the oronym of the other in reverse word order

Rhyme: words that have the same ending sound

Recipe Cards

Tongue twisters and word play form the ingredients for the "recipes" in this word cookbook

Recipe: HIGH FLY AND LIE FLY
Ingredients: fly, high, lie, lye, Bea, be, bee
Directions: Put ingredients in a pot and drizzle in some homophones. Add 3 cups of assonance and read 3 times.

Recipe: FLEA THE FLY AND FLY THE FLEA
Ingredients: Fly, fly, flea, flies, flees, Y's, wise
Directions: Beat Fly, fly, Flea, flies, flees, Y's and wise into a thick cream. Bake 1 cup of homophones and an ounce of circular reasoning in a pan and then top off with the cream. Makes 10 delicious reads.

Recipe: HOLES AND MOLES
Ingredients: holes, moles, alone, a lone, lone, loan
Directions: Blend holes and moles in a batter of alone, a lone, and loan. Beat with homophones, homonyms, oronyms and reverse oronyms and serve lukewarm after a couple of readings.

Recipe: **THE GNU AND THE GNOME**
Ingredients: gnu, new, knew, gnome, Nome
Directions: Boil gnu, new, knew, gnome, and Nome In 1 quart of homophones and assonance and serve hot. Makes 2 readings.

Recipe: RED BOOKS AND BLUE BOOKS
Ingredients: red, read, blue, write, right
Directions: Steam red, read, blue, write and right for 10 minutes and then simmer in a sauce of homophones and heteronyms. Once read to satisfaction, close cover.

Thank you!

I hope you enjoyed the book. Please send any comments, questions, or suggestions to Scott@ScottRavedeBooks.com.

I would greatly appreciate any review you would care to leave at online booksellers. I look forward to exploring the flavor of words with you in my next book.

Cheers!

Scott Ravede

Coming Soon!

Kids Word Cookbook II: *All new tongue twisting recipes to take you to the next level of delicious word play*

Ordering Information

To order additional copies of this book, find out more about Scott Ravede, or get a heads up on his new books, visit www.ScottRavedeBooks.com.

You can also email the author at Scott@ScottRavedeBooks.com.